CAPT.
ARTHUR RAY BROOKS
AMERICA'S QUIET ACE OF W.W.1

by

Walter A. Musciano

HOBBY HELPERS PUBLICATIONS
NEW YORK 61, N. Y.

* * *

ACKNOWLEDGEMENT

The author expresses his sincere appreciation to the Charles Donald Collection for making available the rare photographs which appear in this presentation.

* * *

COVER PAINTING

The cover illustration, reproduced from the original in the Charles Donald Collection, was skillfully executed by the celebrated artist, J. D. Carrick. It depicts the dramatic World War One aerial battle between Arthur Raymond Brooks and eight Fokker D-VII fighters. It was during this encounter that the young American pilot shot down two enemy planes and damaged two others.

* * *

TABLE OF CONTENTS

LIST OF ILLUSTRATIONS

INTRODUCTION

It is unfortunate that in the estimation of all too many followers of World War One aviation, the greatness of an aerial combat Ace is directly proportional to the number of victories with which the flyer is credited. Many Aces passed up larger scores because initially they preferred to help novice pilots get accustomed to warfare aloft and later directed their attention to the welfare and safety of the pilots who served under their command. Valuable Aces of this calibre have been overshadowed by the bizzare and flamboyant "glamour boys"...yet their contribution was a major one. Captain A. Raymond Brooks is typical of such unsung American heroes.

Arthur Raymond Brooks, born in Framingham, Massachusetts on November 1, 1895, was the son of Frank E. Brooks and the former Josephine Levasseur. He discouraged the use of his first name and became known generally as "Ray" Brooks. The future Ace led a normal childhood and attended the public schools of Framingham. The young man exhibited a keen interest in the model airplane building and pursued this hobby for many years. In addition, Ray was fascinated by the history of the conflict between the states and spent considerable time conducting research on the American Civil War.

After his high school graduation Brooks headed for Massachusetts Institute of Technology where he specialized in electrochemical engineering. When Ray was graduated in 1917 with a Bachelor of Science Degree he intended to work for the Bell Telephone Laboratories. But fate decided otherwise...at least for a time. He soon enlisted to fight in the war which was then raging in Europe.

Ray Brooks was ordered to Toronto, Canada, for basic flight training with the Royal Canadian Flying Corps. The trainees lived in tents -- snow covered for most of the 1917-1918 winter. Cadet Brooks was next transferred to Texas where he completed his basic training and was commissioned as a Second Lieutenant in the Aviation Section of the Signal Corps of the United States Army on February 25, 1918.

March 12, 1918 saw the young New Englander on his way to France on board a troopship. He completed advanced training at the Third American Aviation Instructional Center at Issoudon, France, flying French Nieuport 24 fighters. By March 25 Brooks was rated as ready for action and was sent to the Toul sector of the Western Front.

The young Lieutenant, assigned to the 139th Aero Squadron led by Major Augstrom, became part of the third flight under the command of Lieutenant David F. Putnam. Massachusetts born and Harvard educated Putnam had transferred to the 139th from the French Air Service where he had attained the status of an Ace with ten official victories. Putnam was a born leader.

Brooks wrote about Putnam in his diary: "On the assignment to flights I found myself under Putnam and from the time we began operations my admiration grew and my earliest successes were due entirely to such tactics as I learned with this leader."

Ray Brook's first aerial action occurred on June 30, 1918 when Putnam, Brooks and another pilot took off from the 139th Squadron Airfield at Valcoulers on a voluntary patrol. The three S.P.A.D. VII scouts spotted a lone Rumpler two seater and approached it over Vieville-en-Haye. As Putnam swung to the attack the German rear gunner fired furiously and accurately. As Brooks dived upon the enemy craft from its opposite side he was forced to make a split-second decision. Should he shoot the observer or try to destroy the enemy plane?

The average novice in such instance would have aimed unconsciously at a vulnerable spot on the enemy plane in a quick attempt to obtain his first victory. Brooks, however, clearly realized that this enemy gun was a serious danger to his flight leader. So with a short well-placed burst from his single Vickers machine gun he killed the observer and passed up the first of many such potential victories. Putnam then finished off the Rumpler with a long stream of bullets which caused the enemy craft to break up in the air.

This unselfish behavior on the part of Lieutenant Brooks clearly illustrated that the young flyer was more interested in coordinated and organized action and safety of a comrade than in claiming victories at the expense of endangering a fellow pilot.

A short time later, during the big Allied drive on Saint Mihiel, Putnam and Brooks learned through experience that a German flight of three single-seat Fokker D-VII aircraft patrolled the same area every afternoon at the same hour. The trio would not, however, fight over the Allied lines, but always endeavored to entice the S.P.A.D. scouts to chase them towards their own area where, no doubt, the remainder of the Staffel waited unseen for the Americans.

Then one day, while protecting a flight of French artillery-cooperation two-seaters for seventy-five minutes, Brooks and Putnam sighted those three Fokker D-VII scouts and the Americans sped to the attack with such swiftness that the trio was caught by surprise. Putnam engaged the nearest D-VII while Brooks fired at the remaining two. Suddenly, the single Vickers gun on his S.P.A.D. VII jammed. As the two enemy aircraft turned to take advantage of the now helpless Lieutenant he zoomed up into the sun and lost his two adversaries just as his main fuel tank went dry. Ray quickly switched to the eight minute supply of his gravity tank and headed for home with his equally unsuccessful leader who had been shot up by the other German. Both planes landed without a drop of of gasoline in their tanks!

Putnam and Brooks were peeved at their poor showing during this episode and both vowed that they would clobber the taunting Fokkers. Several days later, on July 24, 1918, Putnam was leading Brooks and Lieutenant Fitzkee on patrol along the front lines between Fliry and St. Mihiel when Brooks and Putnam sighted two of the familiar trio and began a long, steep dive. As the Americans approached their quarry the Fokkers turned to the left and began to dive in an evasive maneuver while the Vickers guns began firing.

This time it was Putnam's gun that jammed and he was forced to retire from the fray to watch Ray Brooks fight the two German airmen alone. The possibility of the third Fokker diving from above caused both Americans considerable concern. Brooks remained cool, however, and at three hundred yards opened fire at the nearest D-VII. At that instant his engine choked and sputtered forcing the S.P.A.D. to level off. The young pilot was filled with disappointment. Then the Fokker's wings wobbled and the craft plunged earth-ward. It was a tribute to the amazing accuracy of Brooks short burst at long range!

As the S.P.A.D. assumed level flight its engine revved up just in time to enable Ray to evade an attack from the remaining Fokker which then dived into a cloud bank and escaped. Throughout this battle the third member of the enemy flight remained overhead without realizing that it was a lone S.P.A.D. which had held off two Fokkers and shot down one. Although Brook's victim fell behind the German lines, after several days passed the victory was confirmed.

During the month of July the 139th Aero Squadron was joined by the Lafayette Escadrille under the command of Major William Thaw. This veteran group was undergoing transfer from the French Armee de L'Aire to the American Expeditionary Force and later moved to Vancoulers to become part of the Third Pursuit Group. The 139th Aero Squadron was then joined by the 13th, 22nd, and 49th Aero Squadron and this assembly became known as the Second Pursuit Group.

Arthur Raymond Brooks was transferred to the 22nd Aero Squadron during August 1918 and was promoted to flight leader. His flight was equipped with the more powerful and better armed S.P.A.D. XIII early in September much to Ray's delight. However, he soon discovered that the planes were not too well constructed and his concern for the safety of his men caused him considerable worry. Characteristically, he took action quickly to remedy the faults. Regarding this problem, Brooks observed:

"Supplies were difficult to obtain and the machines were not wholly the best quality, which obliged us to practically rebuild them all. Such things as leaky gas tanks, gritty carburetors, broken bolts, leaky radiators, pipe lines cracked, air pumps broken, water pipe studs broken, machine **gun cams** not functioning, etc., caused us no small amount of worry. Inside of ten days, however, the ships were ready for business and assignments made, and voluntary patrols made to learn the sector immediately started."

Thus the young flight leader trained the green pilots and got the equipment in fighting shape.

Many De Havilland 4 two-seater "battle planes" joined the 22nd Aero Squadron. Brooks flew these on occasion although he preferred the S.P.A.D. scouts.

Brooks and the 22nd moved to the Meuse-Argonne battle front where the Germans had concentrated the most powerful of their Jagdstaffels. During sixty days of action the 22nd Aero Squadron shot down a record number of forty-six enemy aircraft but its own losses were high and this disturbed the consientious Brooks. His concern over these losses is reflected in his writing: "We lost friends and pals who meant as much to us as children to loving parents. Kimber, blown to pieces by a shell; Hudson, killed in a roaring dogfight; Beane, Vernam, Clapp, lost during other hot mixups; one or two others taken prisoners, Agar killed in a crash were our hardest trials."

On September 14, 1918 Flight leader Brooks took off with his men on a mission to protect a Salmson observation two-seater of the 91st Aero Squadron which was returning with valuable reconnaisance information from Conflans. The sky was clear at 2:18 P.M. that Saturday afternoon as the last S.P.A.D wheel left the ground. The six scouts crossed the lines at about 16,000 feet and headed for the rendezvous point East of Flirey. Brooks noted the unusual absence of Allied craft in the sky while observing many German planes of all descriptions. At the appointed rendezvous time of 3:00 o'clock the Salmson failed to appear.

In the distance between Metz and Fresnes Brooks sighted a long string of three groups of aircraft heading in his direction. He identified them a Fokker D-VII scouts consisting of five, six and twelve planes each in a total force of twenty three planes against the six S.P.A.D. pilots. Taking into consideration the fact that their prime objective was the protection of the two-seater which had not yet arrived some of the Americans sped toward the Fokkers hoping to draw them away from the rendezvous point. The twelve plane flight flew around the decoys, however, and slammed into the Brooks formation from above and to the right.

Ray sighted the enemy just as they began the approach and it was too late to warn his squadron mates. As a last resort he turned and raced headlong into the German formation in an attempt to break it up into isolated, less harmful units. His tactic worked but when he emerged from the Fokker formation his squadron mates had disappeared. Suddenly the lone S.P.A.D. was surrounded by eight of the red-nosed enemy and the young American's eleventh aerial battle began. With the odds eight to one against him and ten miles behind the front lines Brooks figured chances of his ever returning to his base were very slim but he was determined to shoot down as many of the enemy as possible before being wiped out. As the young Lieutenant eluded the Spandau gunfire he had visions of his squadron mates destroyed by the fifteen remaining Fokkers.

The uneven battle raged for ten minutes at altitudes which varied from a few hundred feet to three miles. The lone S.P.A.D. side-slipped, spun, looped, and rolled and on several occasions tried to ram the Fokkers. In addition to evading the red-nosed German scouts Brooks gradually worked his way back toward the Allied lines. The American often took advantage of the enemy's numerical superiority by working into positions between the attacking Fokkers so the Germans were in their own way and were forced to withhold their fire.

As one of the D-VII scouts shot by the S.P.A.D., Brooks sped after him firing a short burst which dispatched the German to Valhalla in a tremendous ball of fire. A split second later another Fokker plunged earthward before the exacting aim of the American's twin Vickers guns. With the odds improved six-to-one Brooks was beginning to recognize the enemy's fighting tactics. Then with no warning, the Hispano-Suiza engine coughed and sputtered due to pressure failure in the main gasoline tank. Brooks, was forced to switch to his small, gravity wing tank during certain maneuvers. It was impossible to operate entirely off the gravity tank since it contained only a few minutes fuel supply. The hapless U.S. pilot had to switch back and forth, back and forth as he maneuvered wildly across the sky. At one point, when the propeller almost stopped before the pilot could switch tanks, **a Fokker** quickly moved in on the idling S.P.A.D. to pour a stream of bullets which tore through the windshield, damaged the starboard machine gun — one even grazed the Lieutenant's forehead!

Nearing the Allied lines Brooks got to two more Fokkers with his bullets; they pulled out of the fight and headed for home. So now the odds were four to one. But with only one gun working, his rudder controls damaged, dozens of bullet holes in his plane, plus a sputtering engine, Brooks decided on a last desperate dash for safety. He nosed down his 220-horsepower S.P.A.D. diving with wide open throttle trying to shake off his adversaries. The two Fokkers followed...then only one...this finally turned back as the S.P.A.D. raced over the allied trenches.

The 22nd's field was still some distance away, so Brooks headed for an advanced emergency landing area. The moment after his S.P.A.D. bounced to a landing, Ray raced to a telephone calling his base to learn if any of his men managed to return.

Phil Hassinger, flying rear right in the "Vee" formation, had disappeared — it was feared he had been shot down in the melee. The remarkable Brooks insisted that the lost pilot receive credit for one of the Fokkers Ray had shot down. Brooks' S.P.A.D. was found unflyable, worthy only of salvage. Its rudder cables had been shot away, a tire was punctured, an incendiary bullet had burned itself out in the main spar of the upper wing; a string of bullets had passed through the fuselage a few inches from the pilot's back. The 22nd's Squadron Leader and two of his comrades accompanied Brooks back to the base in a big-brass staff car, the Group Leader insisted Ray take a rest leave.

Lieutenant Howard Clapp had been one of the members of the six-plane flight attacked by the Fokkers. Here are excerpts from a letter he wrote to a close friend regarding the battle:

Tuesday, September 17, 1918

"Last Saturday, my dear friend, Phil, was lost. It was the Old German stunt. Twelve Fokkers attacked our formation of six from above and in the sun. Phil was high rear man and his machine was hit by an explosive bullet...it was blown to bits in midair...

"Brooks had about five after him, and they stuck very tenaciously. But he is a fine flier and a good shot, and, though he fired only 75 rounds during the whole affair, succeeded in bringing down two of them — one in flames. They have both been confirmed, so he is now officially an Ace. He is a corker...

"His machine was badly shot up...in spite of all this he brought the machine safely down in a rough field north of camp.

"...he thought the rest of us in the formation had been destroyed. His nerves were pretty well shot and he has gone away for a few days to rest up. And he insisted that Phil be given a share in the credit for the Boches."

Captain Arthur Raymond Brooks was soon promoted to Commanding Officer of the 22nd Aero Squadron. In October 1918 he was forced to enter a hospital for an operation, before he was ready for return to active duty the Armistice was signed on the eleventh of the following month.

During his short but eventful service on the Western Front, Captain Brooks recalls using four S.P.A.D scout planes. Many pilots gave their aircraft nicknames, usually in honor of their wives or girl friends. Enggaged to Ruth M. Connery, Ray contemplated enscribing her name on his plane. He decided against it because he could imagine the mechanics saying "Ruth needs her nose fixed", or "Ruth's empennage is full of holes", which would not be to his liking. Since Miss Connery was attending Smith College at that time, Brooks named all of his aircraft "Smith".

"Smith I" was the 180-hp S.P.A.D. VII flown by Brooks in the 139th Aero Squadron. "Smith II" was the S.P.A.D. XIII that was shot up in the eight-to-one aerial battle. "Smith III" was wrecked when two spark plugs blew out of the engine during a dogfight, the S.P.A.D. XIII smashed up in a shell hole after a forced landing on the Verdun battlefield. "Smith IV", Captain Brook's last plane of the war, was also flown by Jaques Swaab and Clinton Jones when Ray was hospitalized. This plane was exhibited for many years in the Aviation Building adjoining the Smithsonian Institute in Washington, D.C.

After World War One Ray Brooks remained in the Army Air Corps — unlike the majority of pilots who returned to civilian life. The Captain's decision to continue his military career was prompted by a desire to do his utmost for the newly born Air Service. He considered the airplane a most valuable instrument of war which was about to be shunted aside by the United States Government. This was reflected by the fact that many of our crack squadrons continued to fly French and English aircraft after the war was over. As a high ranking member of the Air Service, Brooks was hopeful of stimulating interest in a strong U. S. Air Force not dependent on other countries for its equipment.

Stationed at Kelly with the 95th Pursuit Squadron, under the command of Field Kindley, Brooks operated British built S.E.5A scouts. After Kindley crashed to his death on February 1, 1920, Reed Chambers was put in command of the 95th Pursuit Squadron. Then Ray became the unit's Commanding Officer when Chambers left the service. A short time later Brooks was promoted to command of the 1st Pursuit Group of the U.S. Army Air Corps. This outfit included the 27th (Diving Hawk insignia), 94th (hat-in-the-ring), 95th (Kicking Mule), and 147th Pursuit Squadrons.

It was on September 25, 1920 that Ruth Connery became Mrs. Arthur Brooks. The couple have a son, Peter.

Brooks left the U.S. Army Air Corps in 1922 to enter the public relations and advertising business which took him to positions in Boston, New York and Florida. In 1925 he became an official of Florida Airways Corporation. The following year saw the young engineer-pilot as associate engineer in the Aeronautics Branch of the U.S. Department of Commerce. He was responsible for the establishment of lighted airways throughout the North-East and worked on emergency fields and beacons and promoting more maintenance facilities. When Ray Brooks had completed this task he was asked to organize and supervise the air operations of the Bell Laboratories.

Flying a Ford Trimotor "Tin Goose" Brooks conducted endless research on air-to-ground radio transmission. Thousands of flights were made and countless parts and electronic assemblies were tested. Brooks' job was to envision the problems involved, then try to solve them. The experiments continued throughout the "thirties" ending in 1939 when the company decided that the task had been completed and sold their research planes. The veteran pilot was assigned to laboratory research for which he was well qualified.

In 1946 Ray transferred to the Bell Telephone Laboratory's public relations staff and became the head of the department in a position he held until his retirement in November 1960. Now Brooks resides in a small suburban northern New Jersey town with his wife.

American Ace Ray Brooks has been the recipient of many top awards including the Distinguished Service Cross, the Silver Star, and Aero Club of America's Medal of Merit. He is a member of the Military Order of World Wars, Founder-Eligible in the Order of Daedalians, Phi Delta Epsilon, Quiet Birdmen, plus numerous other societies.

Captain Brooks is credited in the "official" records with six victories although it is generally agreed that at the minimum his unofficial score was ten. This was due to the difficulty of confirming each victory because most of his aerial battles occurred over German territory thus, verification was often impossible.

And as we have seen, the Ace also devoted much of his time during aerial engagements to close cooperation with the other squadron members in a combined effort to bring down the enemy regardless of who received credit for the "kill".

It was back in August 23, 1919, that Brooks demonstrated his foresight and wise evaluation of military aviation when he wrote:

"Much comment has recently been passed referring to the destruction of U.S. planes in France, but it must be understood that France and England and Italy are all doing the very same thing for the good reason that the ships so destroyed would cost more in overhead expense and upkeep than the price of new ones."

"In England and France the strides made since the war have set the pace for our own country. Our government, in its structure, does not allow one faction to pursue a set course very far without interruption and oftentimes a complete overthrow of plans and consequent wastage, and it is, difficult, therefore, to retain one policy for many years."

"We need an efficient and modern air force, it is in the hands of the Congress whether or not we lead or slump."

"The air service has a hard climb to make, but my belief is that it will reach a position of dignity on its own and one of fruitful co-operation with other branches of the Army if it is given sufficiently encouraging opportunites."

This was penned over four decades ago before many of us were born! Men like Ray Brooks who combine bravery, modesty, and sincerety with the will to fight for a just cause, to win for all, in an unselfish manner are a great credit to the United States. As long as men of this calibre are leaders in our country we will continue our aeronautical and astronautical advances.

It has been said on numerous occasions that A.R. Brooks was a crack shot. He is shown here while attending gunnery school in Toronto, Canada during his basic training with the Royal Canadian Flying Corps. Brooks, seated behind the machine gun, wears a campaign hat with white band to identify him as a cadet.

The bitterness of the cold Canadian winter is indicated by the snow drifts against the tents, the bundled figures of Brooks and a companion as the wind tears at their heavy overcoats. Due to a lack of more suitable facilities the cadets were billeted in the tents shown here.

While mechanics check the rigging of his French Nieuport Scout plane young Brooks stands by patiently at the extreme right. This photograph was taken at Issoudon, France where the American pilots received advanced combat training.

Issoudon, France was the site of a large advanced training center, especially for American pilots. This Nieuport 24 was used by A.B. Brooks to complete his advanced training. Although the Nieuport was a competent fighter plane it was used by the Americans for training in order to prepare the pilots for the more powerful S.P.A.D. machines which they were scheduled to receive.

This photograph was taken on the sidewalk of a small French village located near Brooks' squadron. Notice the laced putees, and the dispatch case. The latter indicates that perhaps the young airman was on a mission of official business.

Standing by the wing tip of his S.P.A.D. VII Ray Brooks checks the progress of the mechanics as they hasten to repair his engine. Flying with the 139th Aero Squadron Brooks was forced down at an emergency landing field due to engine trougle. When the defect was corrected he managed to take off from the rough field with great difficulty.

This craft still sports the French type roundel emblem on the wing.

Twenty-two year old Captain A. R Brooks presents a clean cut figure resplendent in his officer's uniform.

One of the most laudible qualities of the young Ace was his concern over the safety and the well-being of the men under his command. He was especially interested in the novice pilots and generally assisted them with their first "kill". Brooks' objective was to destroy the enemy through a cooperative effort with maximum safety for his men, not to build up a long string of victories for personal glory.

Lieutenant A.R. Brooks is shown seated in one of the S.P.A.D. VII Scouts that he flew during his period of service with the 139th Pursuit Squadron. Notice the stuffed toy "teddy bear" attached to the center of the upper wing which served Brooks as a personal "cootie" mascot. Several Allied as well as German fliers used stuffed animals in this manner during World War One.

This line-up of S.P.A.D. XIII scout planes of the 22nd Aero Squadron was snapped by Captain Brooks. Notice the captured Fokker D-VII at the extreme left of the photograph. Several Allied aircraft still sport the French roundel markings of red-white-blue instead of the red-blue-white of the American Expeditionary Force.

The crude facilities available for engine and airframe repairs at the 22nd Aero Squadron Airfield was typical of all units. Two mechanics near center of photograph overhaul a Hispano-Suiza engine. The S.P.A.D. at right awaits its lower wing which has been removed for repair. This activity was in one of many large tents which serve as repair and storage hangers.

Young Ray Brooks, at right, with a buddy after they were both a-warded the Distinguished Service Cross for gallantry in action. This was but one of several top decorations bestowed upon the American Ace.

Ready for action, S.P.A.D. XIII scouts line up in front of the canvas hangars of the 22nd Aero Squadron in France. The airplane in the center is one of the S.P.A.D biplanes flown by Captain Brooks.

Men of the 22nd Aero Squadron, 2nd Pursuit Group, 1st Pursuit Wing, pose in front of a S.P.A.D. line up on a cold Autumn day in 1918. The "Shooting Stars" was the crack outfit of the 2nd Pursuit Group having attained more victories than any of the other three squadrons in the group.

Captain Ray Brooks poses for a fellow squadron member with his newly acquired moustache. This was removed later but finally allowed to flourish again. A shooting star just above the aviator's wings on his tunic was the insignia of the 22nd Aero Squadron...the men referred to each other as "shooting stars".

On occasion Ray Brooks flew the large two seater De Havilland 4 "battle planes". The Ace is shown after he nosed over during a forced landing on a rough field. Brooks disliked piloting these heavy craft preferring the smaller S.P.A.D.

Another view of the De Havilland 4 piloted by Brooks in which he was forced to make an emergency landing due to mechanical failure. The farmer who owned the field is shown between two of Brook's "rescuers".

During the Allied advances of 1918 the American, French, and English forces occupied numerous installations formerly used by the German military in France. Captain Brooks is seen in front of a building which had been evacuated by retreating Germans. Notice the Iron Cross over the doorway.

This snapshot shows Brooks' last S.P.A.D. "Smith IV", before the shooting star insignia was added. In the background is another S.P.A.D. and a De Havilland 4 with which the squadron was also equipped.

The S.P.A.D. scouts of the 22nd Aero Squadron encountered more German Fokker D-VII scouts than any other single place enemy aircraft. The D-VII, considered to be one of the best single-seat fighters of the first world war, was the only airplane specifically mentioned in the Versailles Treaty. This Fokker, forced down intact by the pilots of the 22nd, is on an American airfield in France. It was eight of these aircraft that surrounded Captain Brooks in one of the epic American battles of the entire aerial war.

Notice the huge canvas-covered hangar at the left.

Ray Brooks (right) talks to a visiting officer in front of the Captain's S.P.A.D. This is the only known photograph taken of Smith "IV" at the front in its final decorations. It was the last S.P.A.D. flown by Brooks in action.

Captain Brook's S.P.A.D. XIII "Smith IV" is seen in the Smithsonian Institution's Aviation Building in Washington, D. C. where it was viewed by millions of visitors for many years.

Little did Ray Brooks dream, when he posed for the photographer, that this S.P.A.D. XIII was destined to be preserved and placed on exhibition at the Smithsonian Institute in Washington, D. C. The "Smith IV" can be seen under the cockpit. Notice that the shooting star insignia had not yet been painted on the fuselage.

Another view of the Brooks S.P.A.D. in the Smithsonian Institution. The XIII, one of the finest scout planes of the 1914-1918 war, was flown by virtually every American Ace including Rickenbacker, Luke, Swaab, and Putnam. It was also one of the strongest airplanes in the conflict.

This piece of aircraft fabric came from one of Captain Ray Brooks'
S.P.A.D. scouts. The stars are white on a blue circle, the tail is orange
and yellow. Entire insignia is outline in white.

Ray Brooks stands before the Eiffel Tower during his visit to Paris before sailing for home after World War One. Like most tourists Brooks was infatuated by the "City of Lights" and saw as many sights as his short leave would permit.

Brooks poses with four buddies on the deck of the troopship which returned the New England Ace to the United States after the war ended. The flyer can be identified at the right by the wings on his tunic.

This German latin cross once was part of a Fokker D-VII shot down
by Captain Brooks when he flew with the 22nd Aero Squadron in 1918.
Notice the bullet hole in the lower portion of the vertical leg.

During the early post-war period Captain A. Raymond Brooks was stationed in the United States with the 22nd Pursuit Squadron flying the same type of equipment as was used during the war. Captain Brooks stands in front of his S.P.A.D. XIII which has had its wartime roundel insignia replaced with the familiar star on the upper right wing.

Captain Brooks at the nose of his post-war stateside S.P.A.D. scout. The flat wartime finish has been replaced with a glossy overall coat of olive drab paint. All the early post-war U. S. Air Service equipment was purchased from England and France. Brooks felt that U. S. manufacturers should be encouraged to develop their own designs instead of our military depending upon imported equipment.

Taken at Kelly Field, Texas in 1919 this photograph shows Brooks in middle row, Weir Cook at extreme right of middle row, and Reed Chambers in top row, second from right. These were some of the most famous flyers who remained in the Air Service after the war's end.

Captain Brooks (third from left) stands with members of his flight at Kelly Field, Texas in 1919. The British S.E.5A scout planes of the 95th Pursuit Squadron in the background have the "kicking mule" insignia on their fuselage.

S.E.5A Scout planes of the 95th Pursuit Squadron fly in formation over Kelly Field, Texas on February 1, 1920. Brooks was a member of this formation as was Squadron Leader Field Kindley who crashed to his death shortly after this photograph was taken.

This S.E.5A of the 95th Pursuit Squadron is flown by Lieutenant Stanley Ames, one of Captain Brooks' squadron members. This photograph was taken by Brooks as his squadron flew in review over Kelly Field. It was during this fly-by that Kindley crashed.

Captain Brooks with his commanding officer and a line up of S.E.5 fighters of the 95th Pursuit Squadron at Kelly Field, Texas in 1919. Captain Reed Chambers, also an American Ace of renown, stands at the left. When Chambers left the Air Service Brooks was selected to lead the famous Pursuit Squadron.

Of special interest to marking buffs and model builders are those dazzling red-white-blue stripes on the fin, elevator, stabilizer, and fuselage rear.

Captain A. R. Brooks, Commanding Officer of the First Pursuit Group which included four crack squadrons, stands alongside his S.E.5A Scout. This craft was assigned to the 95th Pursuit Squadron based at Kelly Field, Texas; the "Kicking Mule" squadron insignia is clearly shown.

The World War One American Ace as he appeared in 1960 when he re-
tired from the Bell Telephone Laboratories as chief of its public relations
staff. Brooks' post-war civilian activities included airways engineering
for the U.S. Department of Commerce, aviation public relations work, as
well as electrical engineering.

PHOTO BY HOWARD LEVY

Most recent photograph of Ray Brooks was taken during the planning sessions for the World War One Flyers Reunion at Wright-Patterson Air Force Base in Dayton, Ohio, June 21 to 25, 1961. Brooks was a guest of the U.S. Air Force Museum along with 327 other World War One flyers including Aces Reed Chambers, Eddie Rickenbacker and Clayton Bissell.

This reunion was climaxed with an air show featuring rebuilt SPAD, Nieuport, Pfalz, Fokkers and other immortal World War One aircraft.

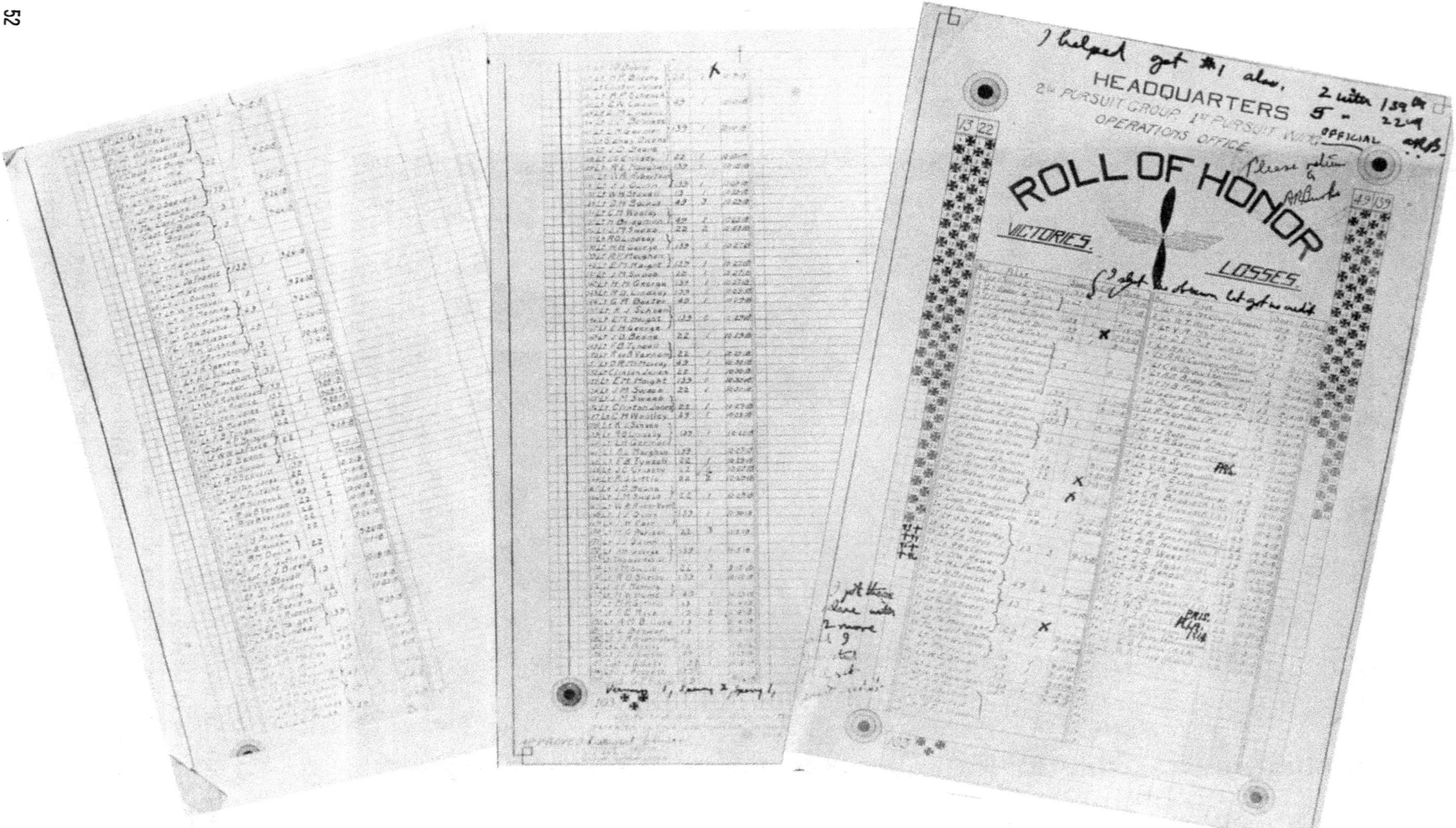

The Second Pursuit Groups Roll of Honor shown here is an unusual "find" for the World War One enthusiast interested in the records prepared in France during the conflict. The ink script additions were made by Cap-

22ND. AERO SQUADRON

RAY CLAFLIN BRIDGMAN
CAPTAIN
COMMANDING

HONOR ROLL.

VICTORIES PILOT		DATE	E.A.	VICTORIES PILOT	DATE	E.A.	LOSSES PILOT		DATE
LT. BROOKS	✓	SEPT. 2	✱	LT. SWAAB			LT. McCORMICK	KIA.	SEPT.
LT. BROOKS	✓			LT. JONES	OCT. 27	✱	LT. HASSINGER		SEPT.
LT. JONES		SEPT. 4	✱	LT. SWAAB			LT. KIMBER	KIA.	SEPT.
LT. TYNDALL				LT. BEANE	OCT. 29	✱	LT. SPERRY		OCT. 4
CAPT. BRIDGMAN	✓	SEPT. 12	✱	LT. LITTLE	OCT. 29	✱✱	LT. HUDSON	KIA.	OCT. 5
LT. BROOKS	✓	SEPT. 14	✱✱	LT. CRISSEY	OCT. 29	✱✱	LT. AGAR (died of injuries)		OCT. 30
LT. HASSINGER				LT. TYNDALL	OCT. 29	✱	LT. BIGGS		OCT. 27
CAPT. BRIDGMAN				LT. RORISON	NOV. 3	✱✱✱	LT. BEANE	KIA.	OCT. 30
LT. HUDSON		SEPT. 24		LT. SWAAB	SEPT. 8	✱✱✱	LT. VERNAM	KIA.	OCT. 30
LT. LITTLE							LT. TIFFANY (prisoner)		NOV. 3
LT. SPERRY		OCT. 4	✱	LT. SPERRY	SEPT. 24	++	LT. GIBSON	KIA.	NOV. 3
LT. HUDSON							LT. CLAPP		NOV. 3
LT. DOOLIN		SEPT. 26	✱	LT. SPERRY	OCT. 4	+			
LT. BEANE		SEPT. 26	✱				8 Killed		
LT. JONES		SEPT. 28	✱✱	LT. VERNAM	OCT. 30	+	2 Missing		
LT. HUDSON		SEPT. 28	✱				2 Prisoners		
LT. TYNDALL		SEPT. 28	✱			46	12		
CAPT. BRIDGMAN									
LT. LAFORCE		SEPT. 28	✱						
LT. BEANE									
LT. SWAAB		SEPT. 28	✱						
LT. JONES		OCT. 9	✱						
LT. VERNAM		OCT. 10	99						
LT. SWAAB		OCT. 23	✱✱						
LT. VERNAM		OCT. 18	✱						
LT. JONES		OCT. 18	✱						
LT. GRYLLS		OCT. 18	✱						
LT. BEANE									
LT. JONES	✓	OCT. 9	✱						
LT. BROOKS									
LT. BEANE									
LT. CRISSEY		OCT. 10	✱						
LT. SWAAB		OCT. 27	✱						
LT. BEANE		OCT. 29	✱						
LT. TYNDALL									
LT. VERNAM		OCT. 29	✱						
LT. JONES		OCT. 30	✱						
LT. SWAAB		OCT. 31	✱						

Sept 2, 1918 to Nov. 3, 1918

46 official victories
R.C.B.
May 21, 1919

My official victories alone were 4
" Total " " 6
or counting 1 with Putnam 7
5 with 22nd 2 w. 139th
9 or 10 unofficial total
R.C.B.

Another item of extreme interest, an unusually rare document, is the
22nd Aero Squadron Honor Roll. Again, also, the notations in script were
by Captain Brooks.

CAPTAIN A. R. BROOKS' NIEUPORT 24

The inexperienced pilots of the American Expeditionary Force, when they arrived in France, were rushed through combat training at several centers. One of the most important instruction units was located at Issoudon; it was here that Ray Brooks received his fighter training. One of the most popular aircraft used for this purpose by the Americans was the tiny French Nieuport 24.

A descendant of the famous, successful Nieuport 11 and 17 scouts designed by Gustave Delage, the 24 was decidedly more streamlined, faster, and powerful. It was employed by the armed forces of England and France; two hundred and sixty one type 24 aircraft were purchased by the United States for training work. The Nieuport 24 outclassed by the contemporary German and Allied designs, never attained the prominence and popularity of its ancestors. Yet numerous Aces, including the French hero Nungesser, indicated a preference for the plane over the newer and stronger S.P.A.D.

Maximum speed for the fighter-trainer was 116 miles per hour; the airplane could climb to 16,400 feet in just over twenty one minutes. Its service ceiling was 18,200 feet. A 130 horsepower Le Rhone rotary engine powered the 1,200 pound craft.

Standard armanent consisted of a single Vickers machine gun mounted off-center on the fuselage top. Many British Nieuports were fitted with a Lewis machine gun mounted above the upper wing. The single gun installation was not very effective against the twin guns of most German craft.

Standard color scheme of the Nieuport 24 was silver; only a very few were camouflaged at the front.

United States training Nieuports sported huge numbers on the fuselage sides as a means of positive identification and flew with either American or French national insignia roundels.

The three-view drawings show French roundels on the wings.

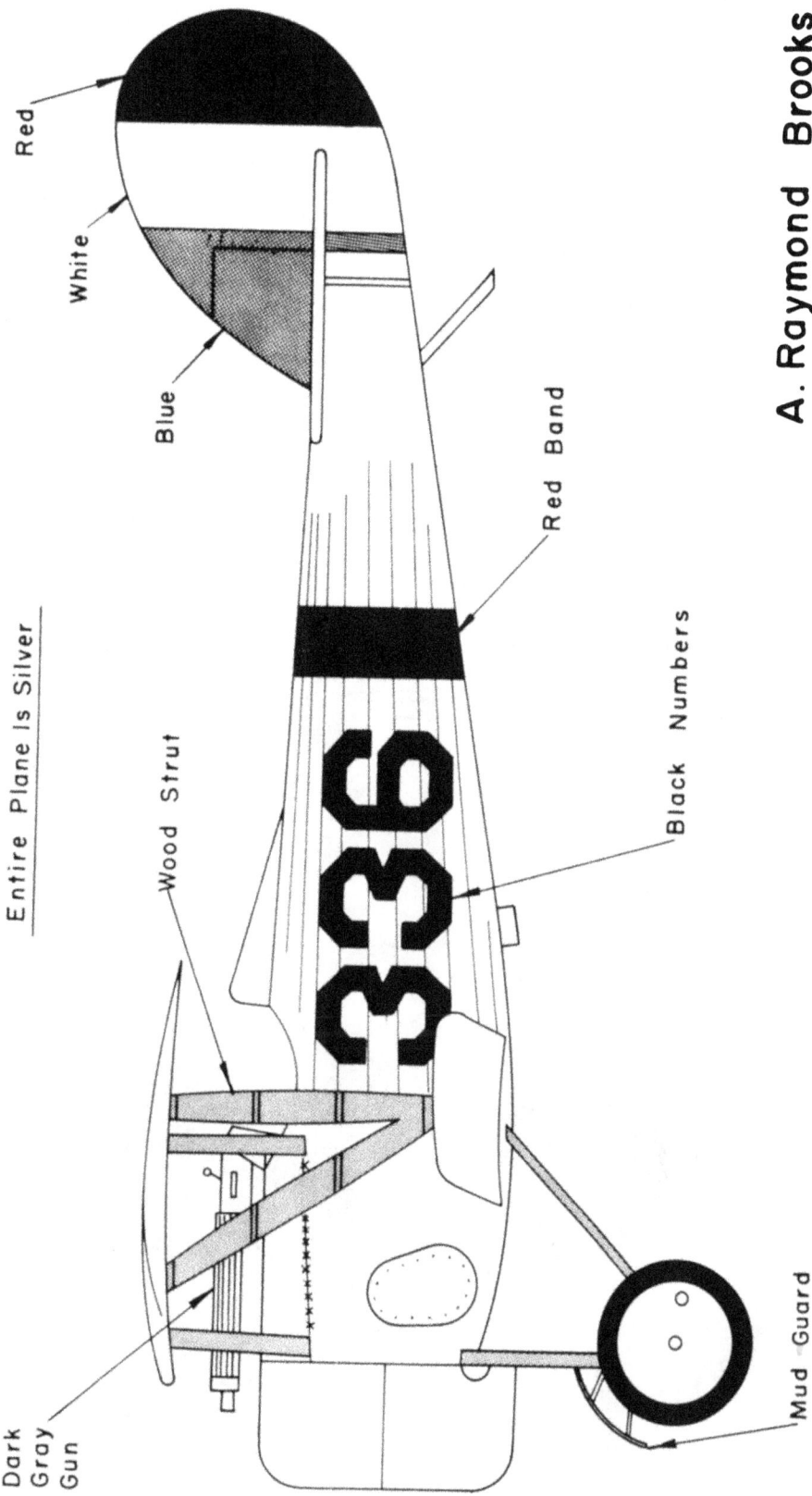

Red

White

Blue

Entire Plane Is Silver

Wood Strut

Red Band

Black Numbers

336

Dark
Gray
Gun

Mud Guard

A. Raymond Brooks
Issoudon
Nieuport 24

Red

White

Blue

Red Band

A. Raymond Brooks
Issoudon
Nieuport 24

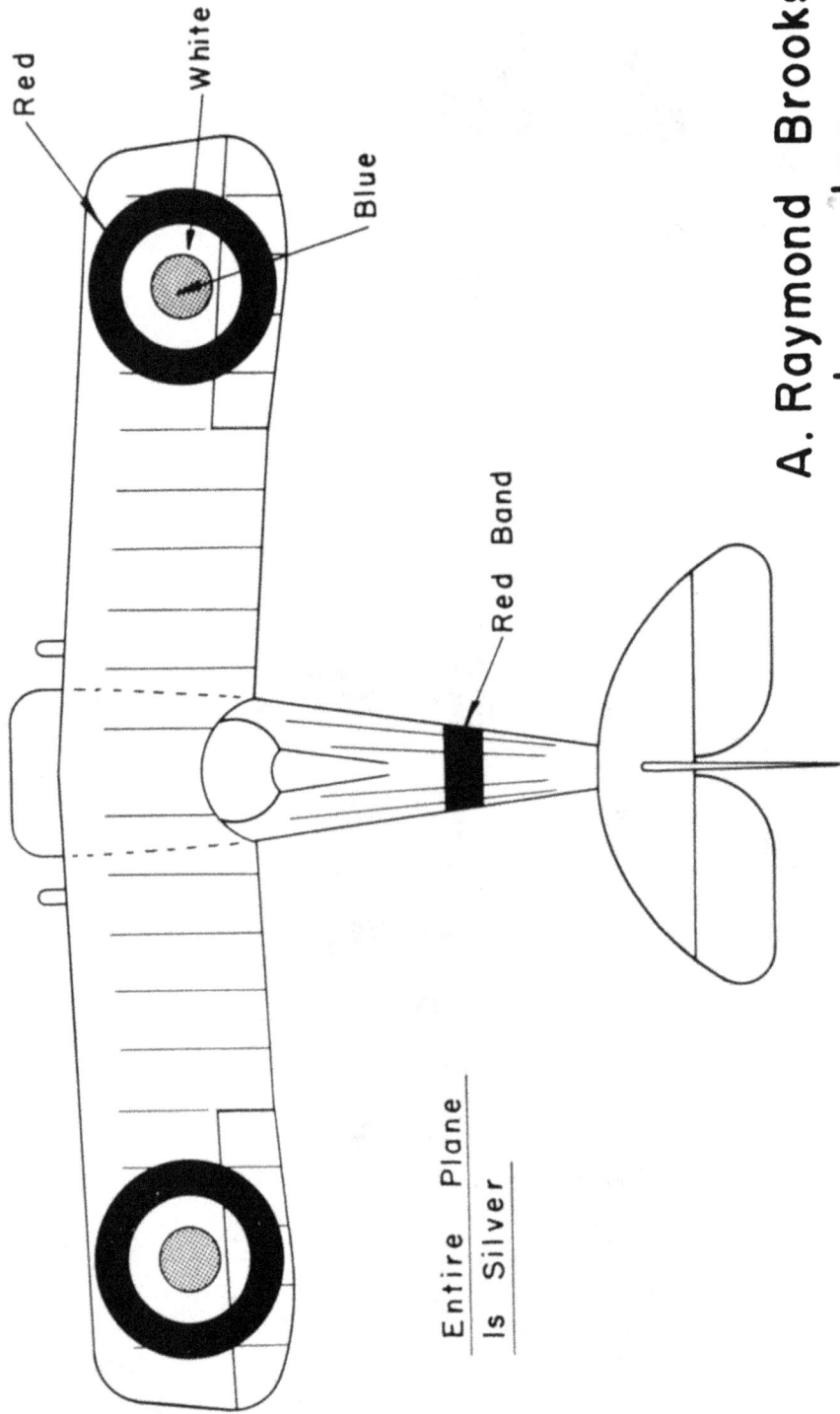

Entire Plane
Is Silver

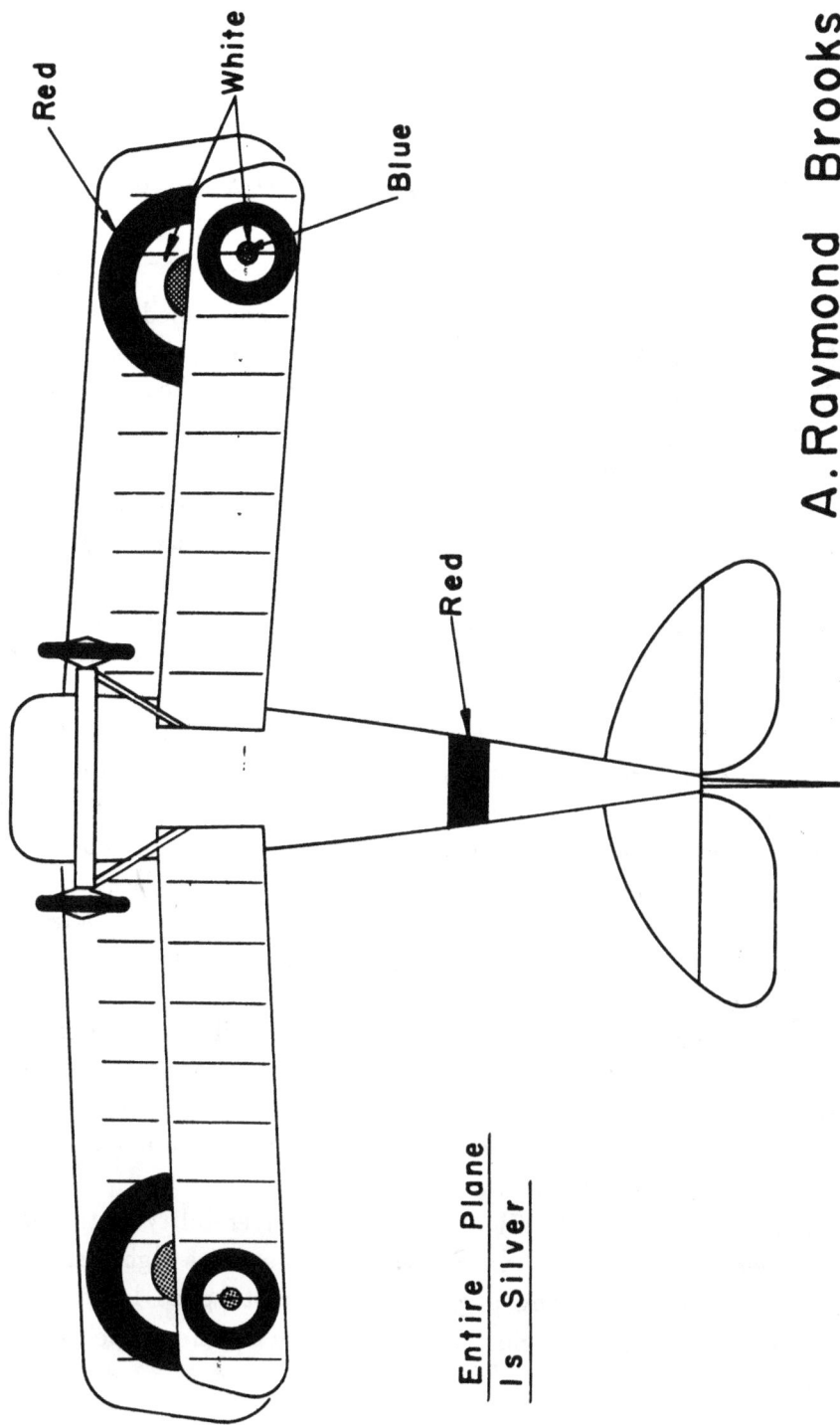

Red

White

Blue

Red

A. Raymond Brooks
Issoudon
Nieuport 24

Entire Plane
Is Silver

CAPTAIN A. R. BROOKS' S.P.A.D. VII

In December 1917 the United States Government purchased one hundred and eighty-nine S.P.A.D VII scout planes from France. This is the single seat fighter that Ray Brooks flew with the 139th Aero Squadron in the summer of 1918.

M. Becherau designed the S.P.A.D. VII in late 1915; it reached the front in quantity by the Autumn of 1916. The fighter, an immediate success, was flown by the French, English, Italian, Russian, Belgian, and American air arms. Many famous Aces including Georges Guynemer, Rene Fonck, and Francesco Baracca flew to victory in this famous machine. The name of S.P.A.D. stood for the initials of its maker, Societe Pour Aviation et ses Derives.

With one hundred and eighty horsepower Hispano-Suiza eight-cylinder, water-cooled engine the plane attained a maximum speed of 119 miles per hour at 6,500 feet. The 1,550 pound fighter was able to climb to 9,800 feet altitude in eleven and one half minutes. Its ceiling was 18,000 feet. Enough fuel was carried for a flight of seventy-five minutes duration.

Standard armament was a single Vickers machine gun mounted atop the engine cowl. Some English S.P.A.D. scouts were also fitted with a Lewis gun atop the upper wing.

The early French Armee de L'Aire's S.P.A.D. VII scouts were painted a silvery-gray overall; however, by the time the Americans arrived on the scene the French established a system of olive green, tan, and light gray camouflage which the American Expeditionary Force also adopted for use on U.S. operated aircraft.

Although the S.P.A.D. VII lacked the maneuverability of the earlier Nieuport designs it proved a superior airplane due to its higher speed and tremendous strength. Gliding angle was rather steep so landings were made with considerable engine power to maintain the proper angle of approach.

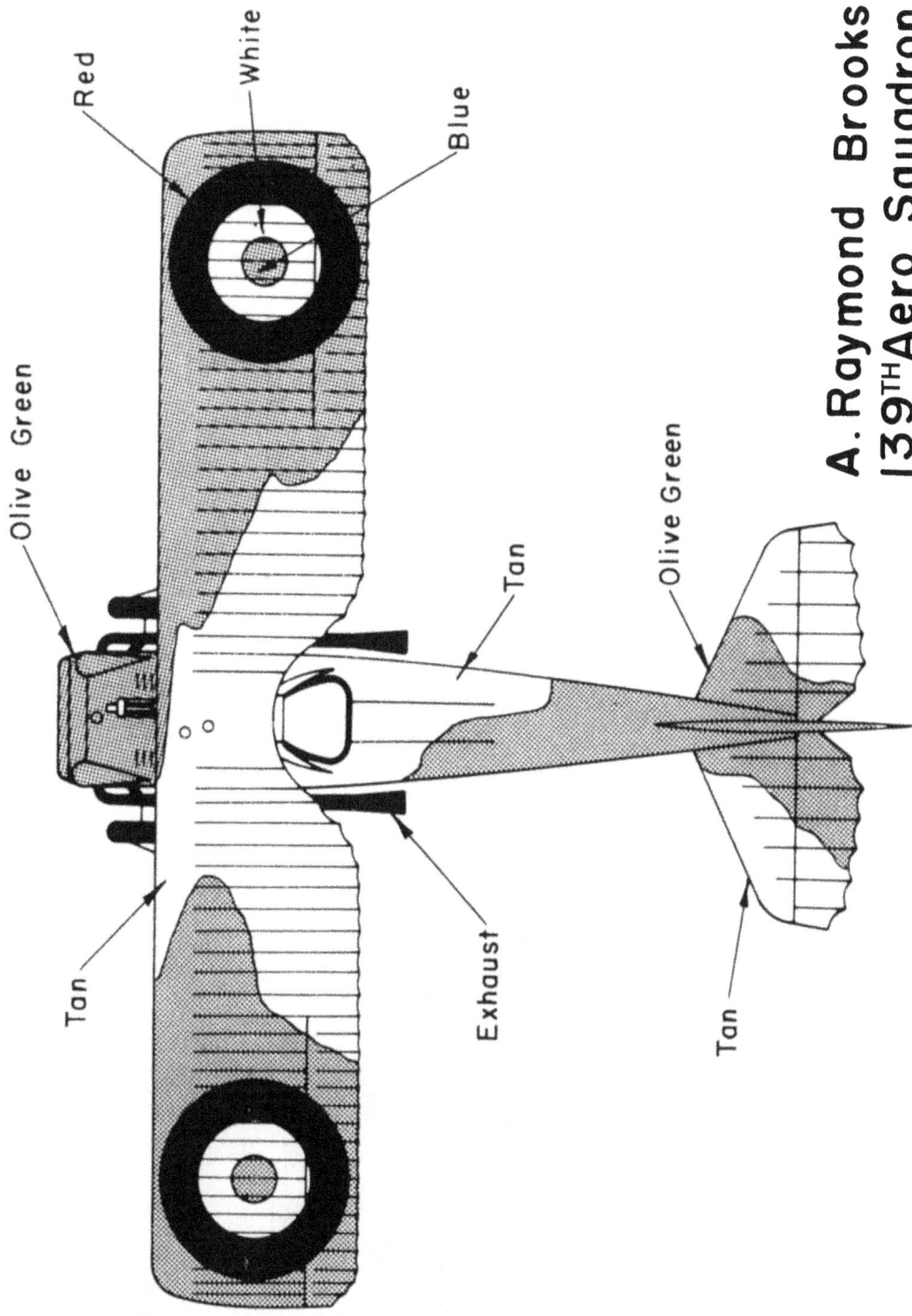

Red

White

Blue

Olive Green

Tan

Tan

Exhaust

Olive Green

Tan

A. Raymond Brooks
139TH Aero Squadron
S.P.A.D. VII

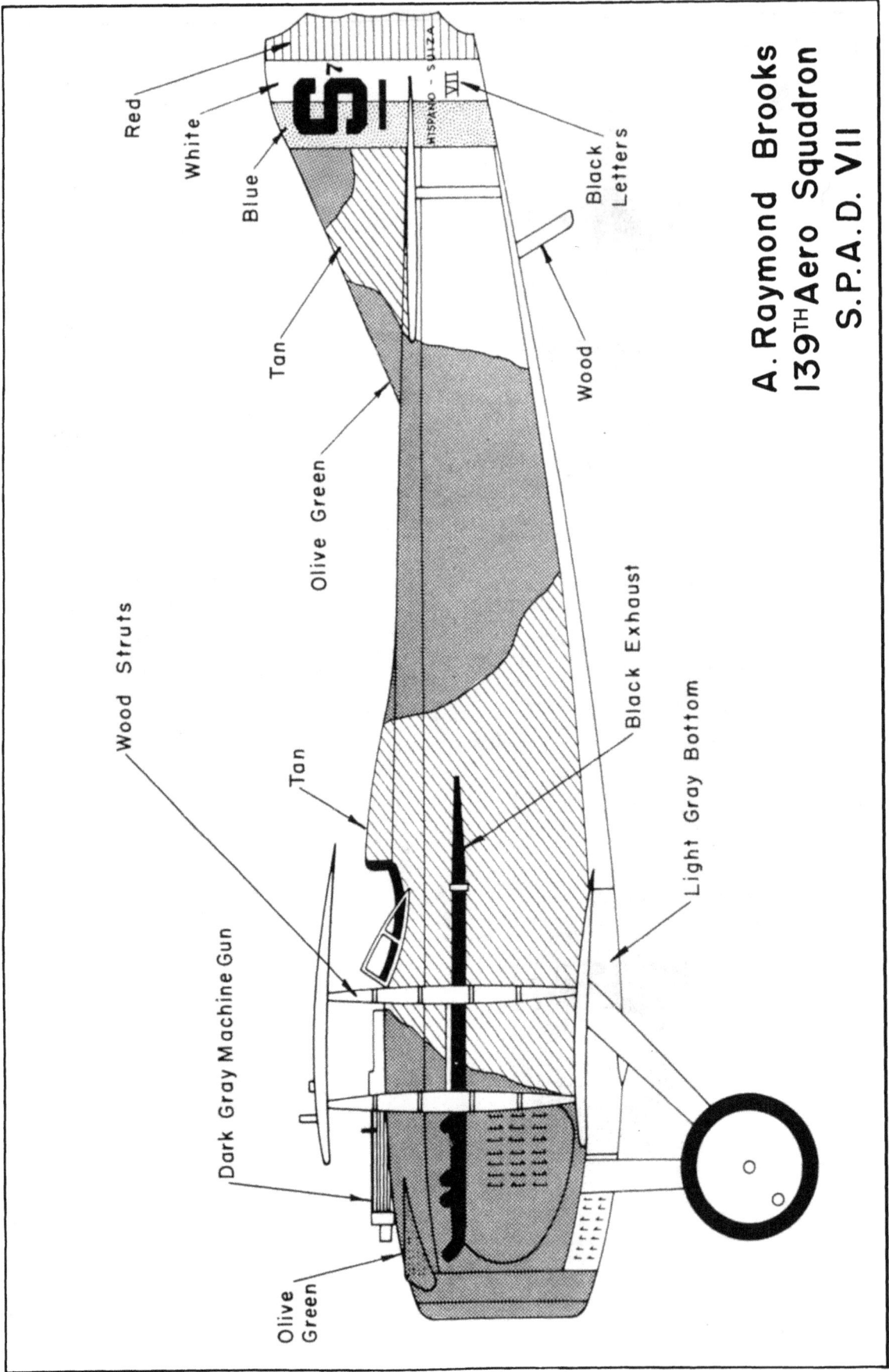

Red

White

Blue

Tan

Olive Green

Wood Struts

Tan

Dark Gray Machine Gun

Olive Green

HISPANO - SUIZA

VII

Black Letters

Wood

Black Exhaust

Light Gray Bottom

A. Raymond Brooks
139TH Aero Squadron
S.P.A.D. VII

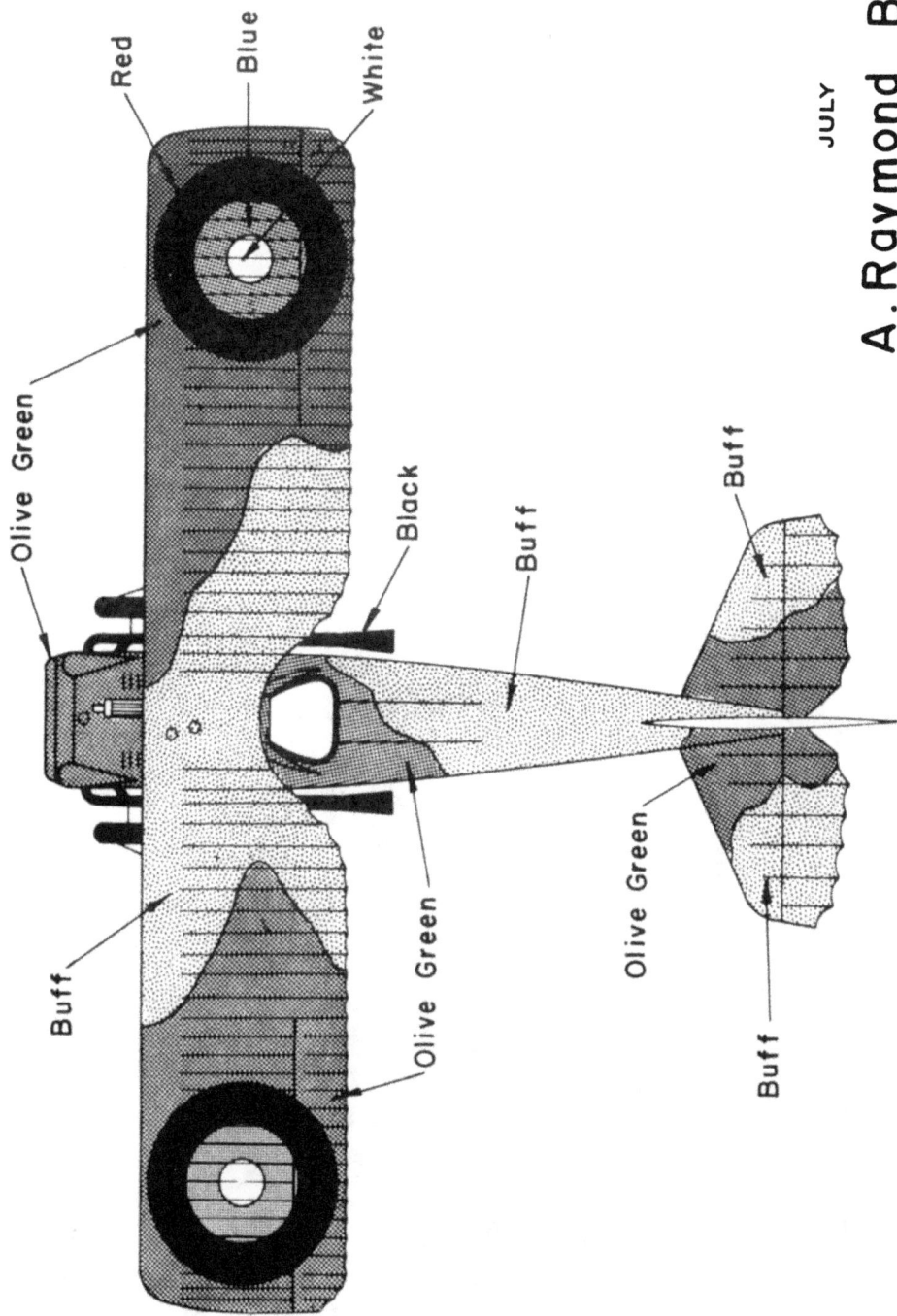

Red

Blue

White

Olive Green

Black

Buff

Buff

Olive Green

Buff

Olive Green

Buff

JULY

A.Raymond Brooks
139 Aero Squadron
S.P.A.D. VII

61

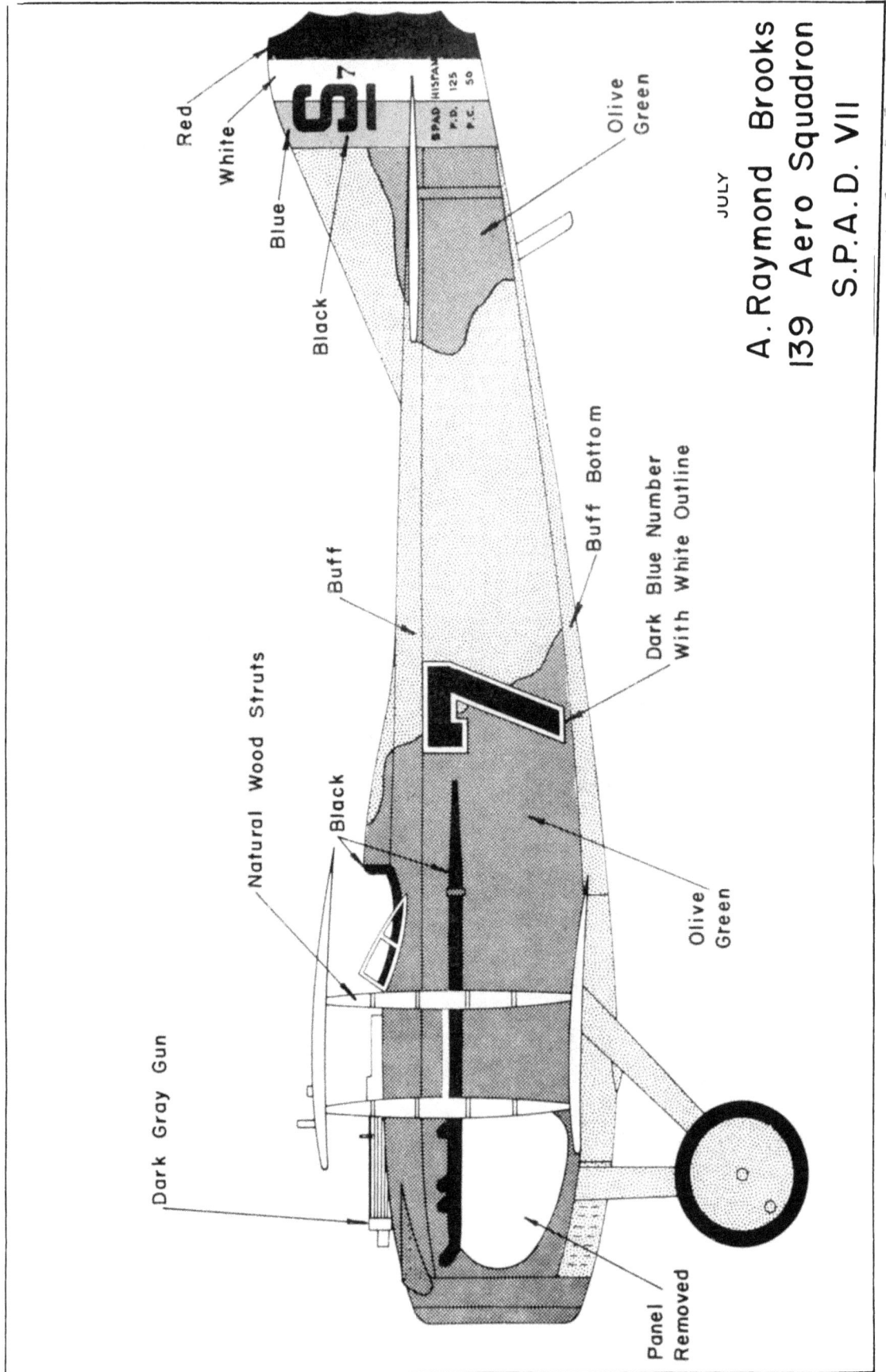

Red

White

Blue

Black

S 7

SPAD HISPANO
P.D. 125
P.C. 50

Olive
Green

Buff

Natural Wood Struts

Black

Buff Bottom

Dark Blue Number
With White Outline

Olive
Green

Dark Gray Gun

Panel Removed

JULY

A. Raymond Brooks
139 Aero Squadron
S.P.A.D. VII

CAPTAIN A. R. BROOKS' S.P.A.D. XIII

One year after the S.P.A.D. VII designs were completed type XIII was born. This, a more powerful and larger development of the earlier type VII, was considered even more successful. The XIII gradually replaced the early disign in the French Escadrilles during the fall of 1917; 8,472 S.P.A.D. XIII machines were built by nine manufacturers under license.

In March of 1918 the United States purchased 893 S.P.A.D. XIII scouts from the French Government. This was the type flown by Brooks when he joined the 22nd Aero Squadron in late summer of 1918. The majority of American Aces flew the type XIII including Rickenbacker, Luke, Swaab, and Jones. Sixteen American Squadrons were equipped with the S.P.A.D. XIII and this fighter proved very popular in the A.E.F.

A Hispano-Suiza eight cylinder engine of two hundred horse-power gave the S.P.A.D. XIII a top speed of 130 miles per hour at 6,500 feet altitude. The craft could climb to 16,400 feet in twenty minutes; its ceiling was 22,300 feet. Gross weight of the XIII was 1,815 pounds. Some versions were fitted with a 235 horsepower engine.

Two Vickers machine guns were buried in the upper cowling. In addition, two small 25-pound Cooper bombs could be carried in the fuselage behind the pilot's seat. Some experiments were conducted with cannon installations on modified S.P.A.D. VII and XIII frames. These were abondoned due to the fumes which entered the cockpit and nauseated the pilot as well as the weapon's slow rate of fire.

S.P.A.D. XIII scouts in the A.E.F. sported a more complex camauflage pattern than the earlier type VII. Brown, Tan, Dark Green, Light Green , and Light Gray were used as the accompanying drawings illustrate.

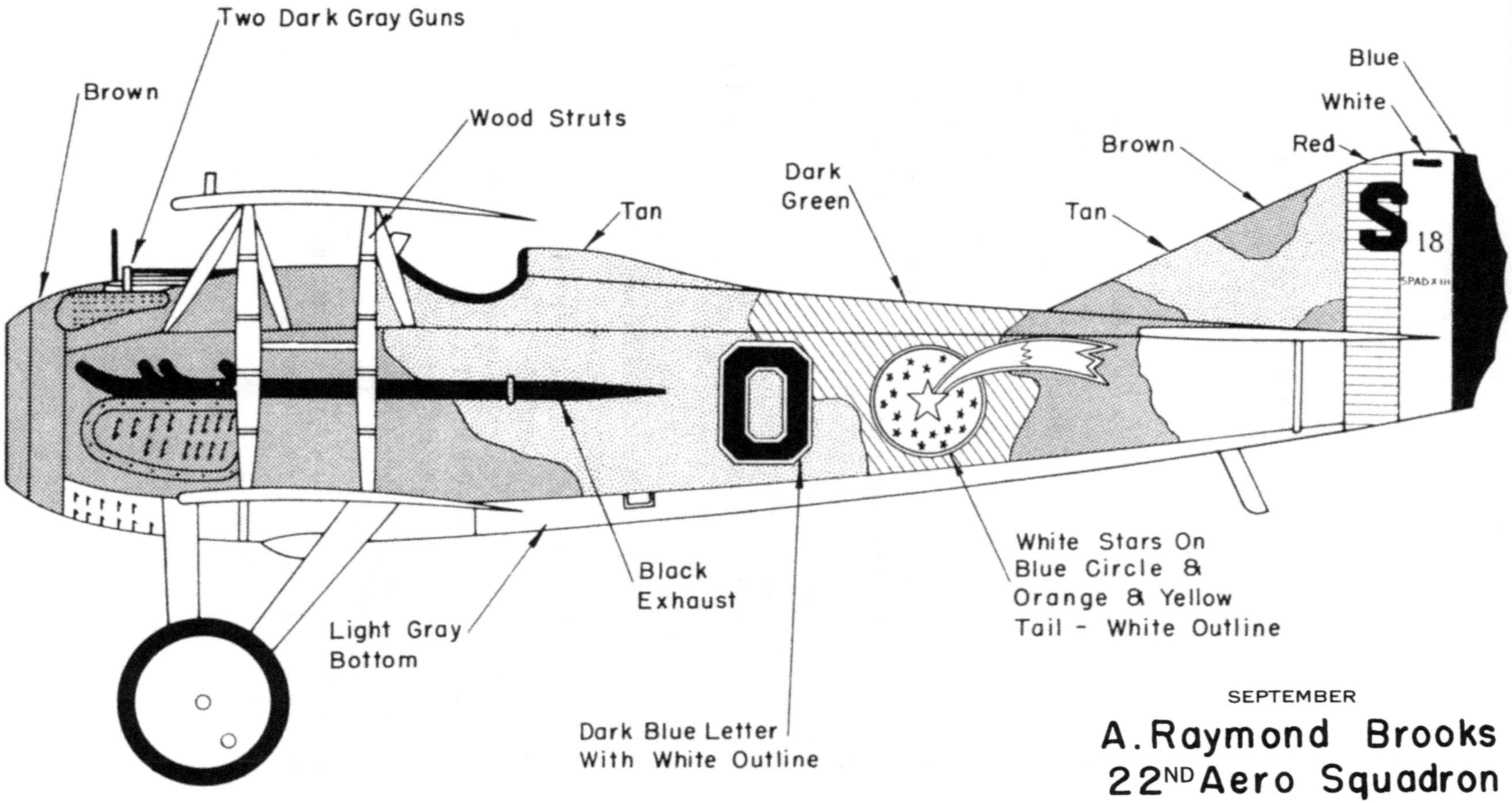

Blue
White
Red
Brown
Tan

SEPTEMBER

A. Raymond Brooks
22ND Aero Squadron
S.P.A.D. XIII

S 18
S.P.A.D X III

White Stars On
Blue Circle &
Orange & Yellow
Tail - White Outline

Dark Green

Tan

Wood Struts

Two Dark Gray Guns

Brown

Black Exhaust

Dark Blue Letter
With White Outline

Light Gray Bottom

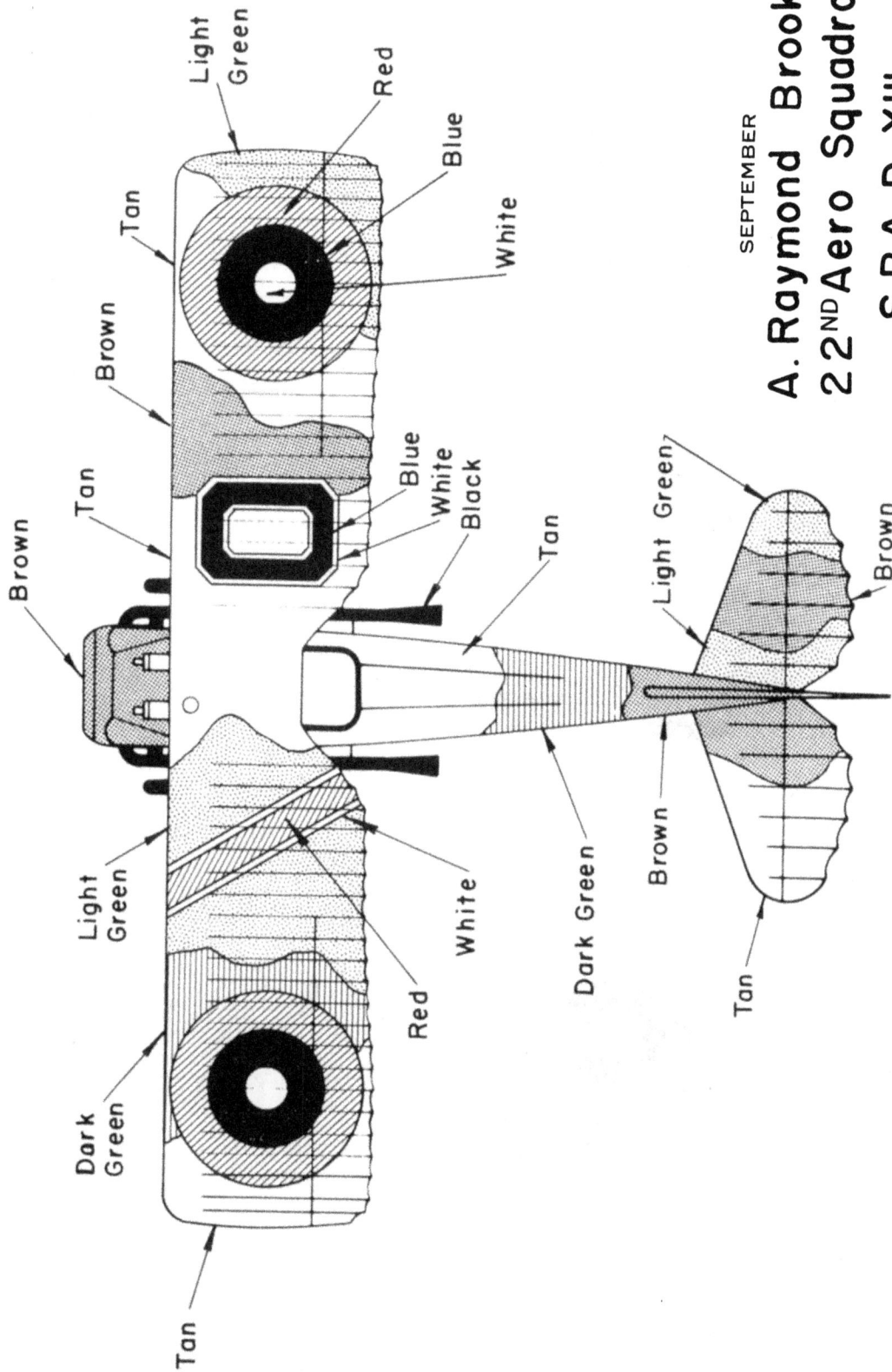

Light
Green

Red

Blue

White

Tan

Brown

Tan

Blue
White
Black

Brown

Tan

Light
Green

Brown

Tan

Light
Green

Red

White

Dark Green

Brown

Dark
Green

Tan

Tan

SEPTEMBER

A. Raymond Brooks
22ND Aero Squadron
S.P.A.D. XIII

65

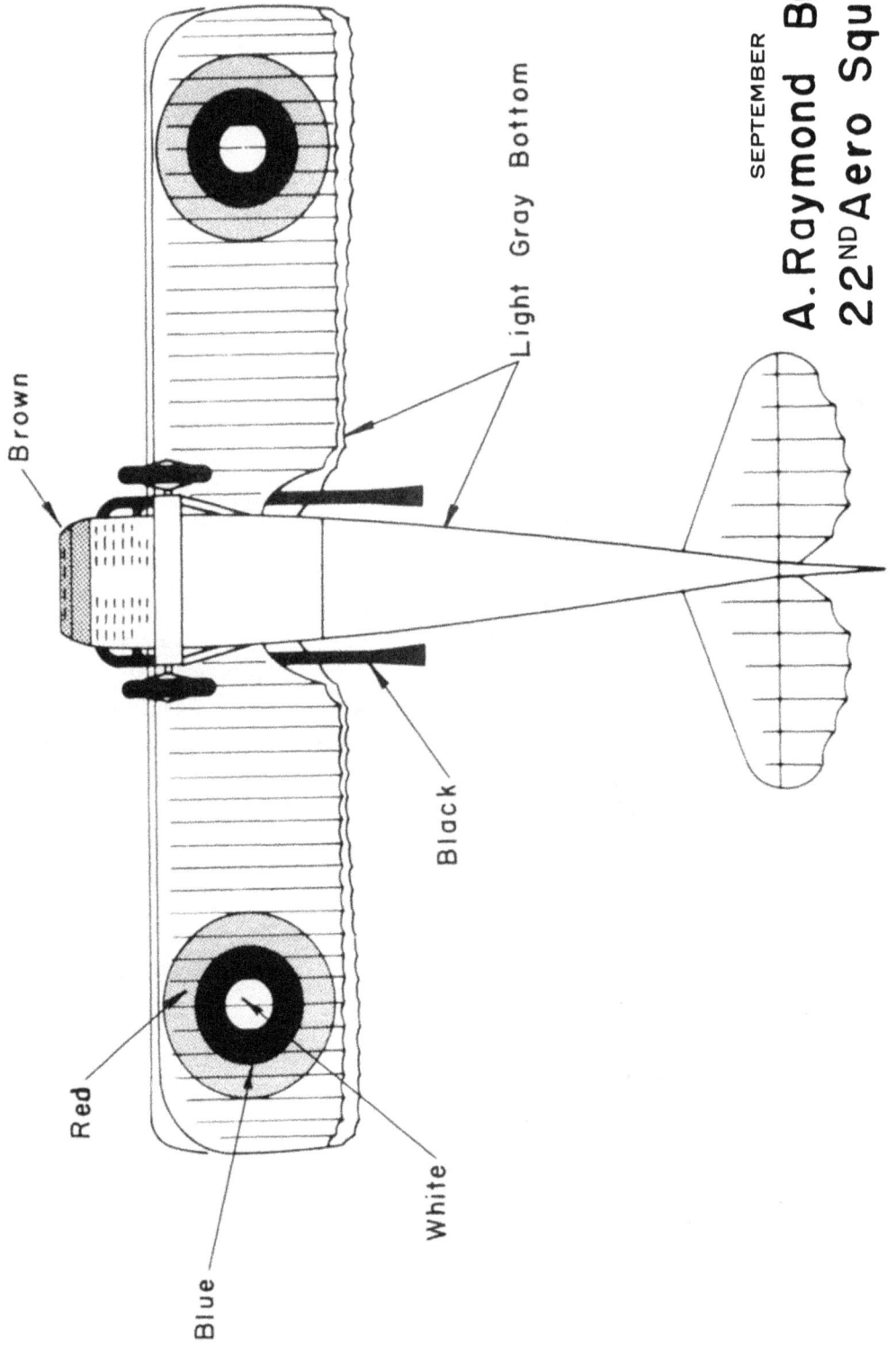

Brown

Light Gray Bottom

Black

Red

Blue

White

SEPTEMBER

A. Raymond Brooks
22ND Aero Squadron
S.P.A.D. XIII

66

Blue
White
Red

XIII
76
S
2
220
45
40
PU- 1
PC- 1

Brown

Tan

Black

Brown

White Stars On
Blue Circle &
Orange & Yellow
Tail — White Outline

OCTOBER
A. Raymond Brooks
22ND Aero Squadron
S.P.A.D. XIII

Blue With White
Outlines

Dark Green

Tan

20

Wood Struts

SMITH IV

Black
Exhaust

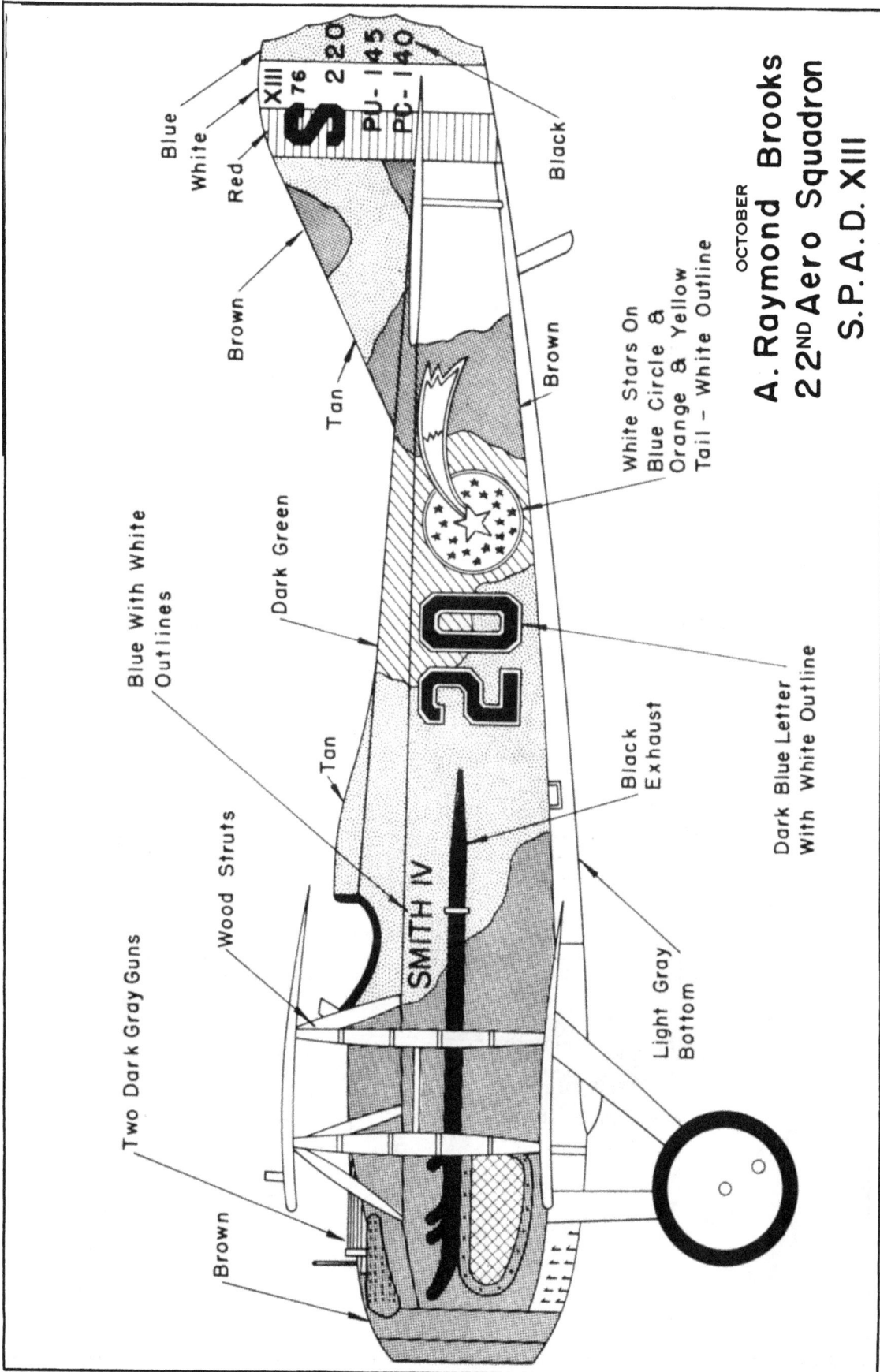

Two Dark Gray Guns

Dark Blue Letter
With White Outline

Light Gray
Bottom

Brown

'67

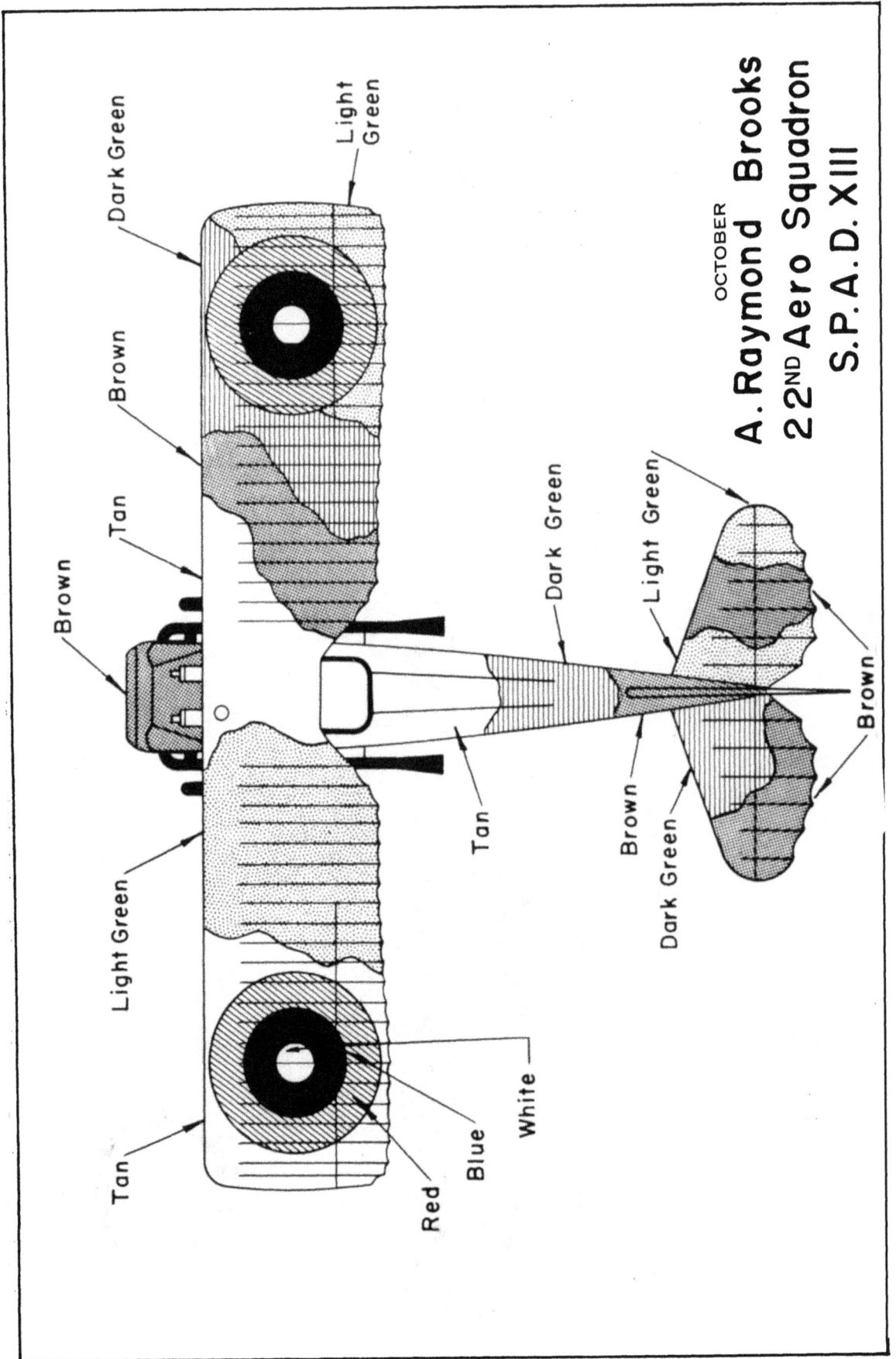

Dark Green

Light Green

Brown

Tan

Brown

Light Green

Tan

Red

Blue

White

Dark Green

Light Green

Brown

Brown

Dark Green

OCTOBER
A. Raymond Brooks
22ND Aero Squadron
S.P.A.D. XIII

68

CAPTAIN A. R. BROOKS' S.E.5A

When Ray Brooks returned to the United States after the end of World War One he elected to remain in the air service. He was soon transferred to the 95th Pursuit Squadron where, before long, he became squadron commander and then group commander. During those post war years the 95th was equipped with the English built S.E.5A scout planes.

The S.E.5A, developed by the British Government at its Royal Aircraft Factory, was designed by the team of Major F.W. Gooden, H.P. Folland, and J. Kenworthy. The initials of the craft mean Scouting Experimental 5, modification A. The airplane was unquestionably one of the most successful designs of the entire war.

The first of over five thousand S.E.5 machines appeared in December 1916, by Spring 1917 they were in action on the Western Front. The design was very stable and easy to fly. Many Aces including McCudden, Mannock, Bishop, Springs, Ball, and Beauchamp-Proctor piloted the S.E.5 to numerous victories. Armament included one Vickers machine gun imbedded in the upper cowl and synchronized to fire through the propeller arc. In addition, a light weight Lewis machine gun was fitted on a moveable mount above the upper wing. This could be aimed forward or upwards at a steep angle.

Originally employing a 150 horsepower Hispano-Suiza eight cylinder engine the final S.E.5A was equipped with a 200 horsepower Wolseley Viper engine. Maximum speed of the craft was 137 miles per hour at sea level and 126 miles per hour at 10,000 feet. An altitude of 15,000 feet could be reached in 19.5 minutes. Gross weight was 1.940 pounds.

The S.E.5A, a strong airplane, was comparably fast and decidedly superior to the majority of German designs of the day. Only the vaunted Fokker D-VII could be compared with the never-to-be-forgotten S.E.5A..

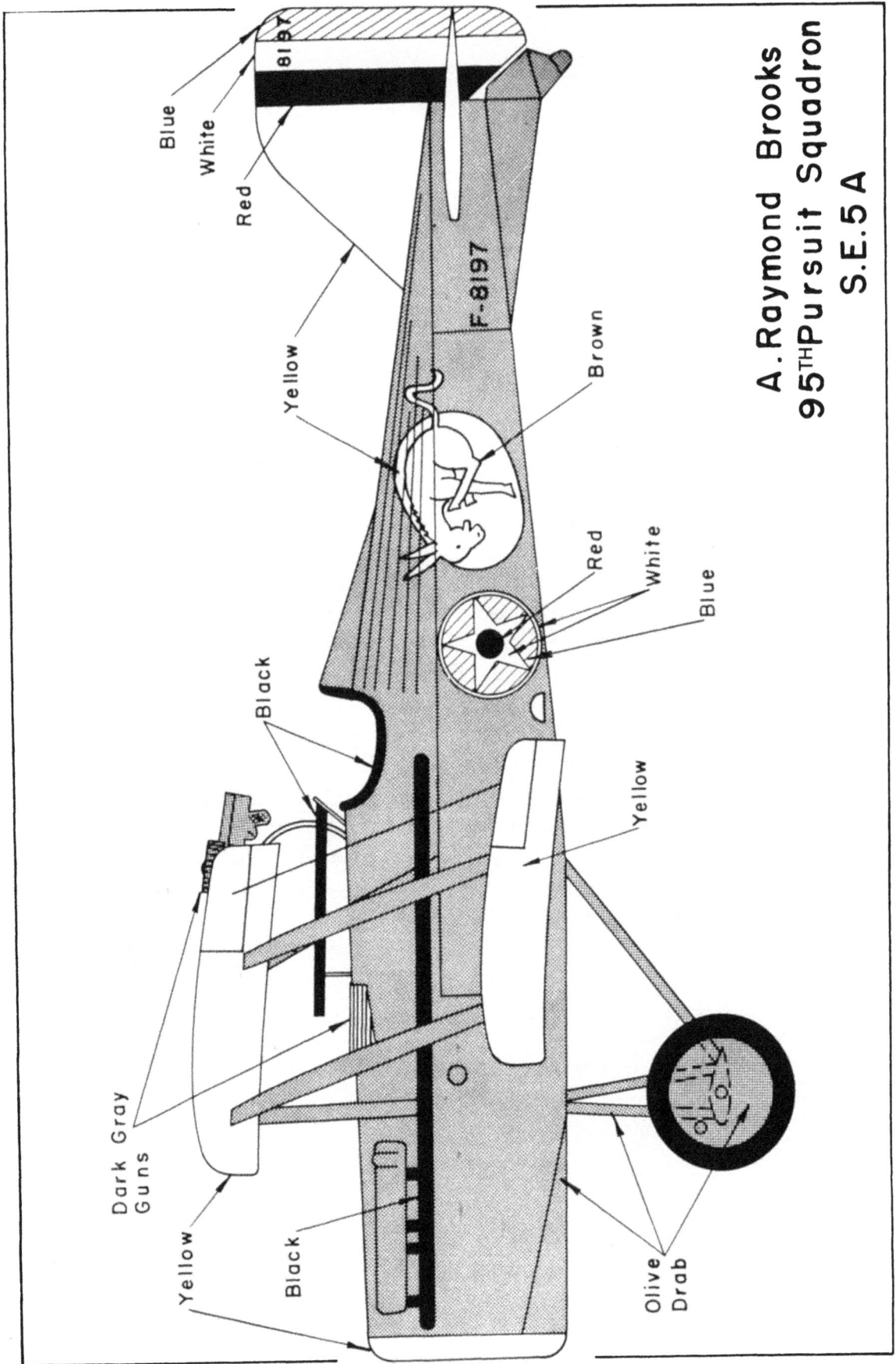

A.Raymond Brooks
95TH Pursuit Squadron
S.E.5A

Blue
White
Red
Yellow
F-8197
Brown
Red
White
Blue
Black
Yellow
Dark Gray
Guns
Yellow
Black
Olive
Drab

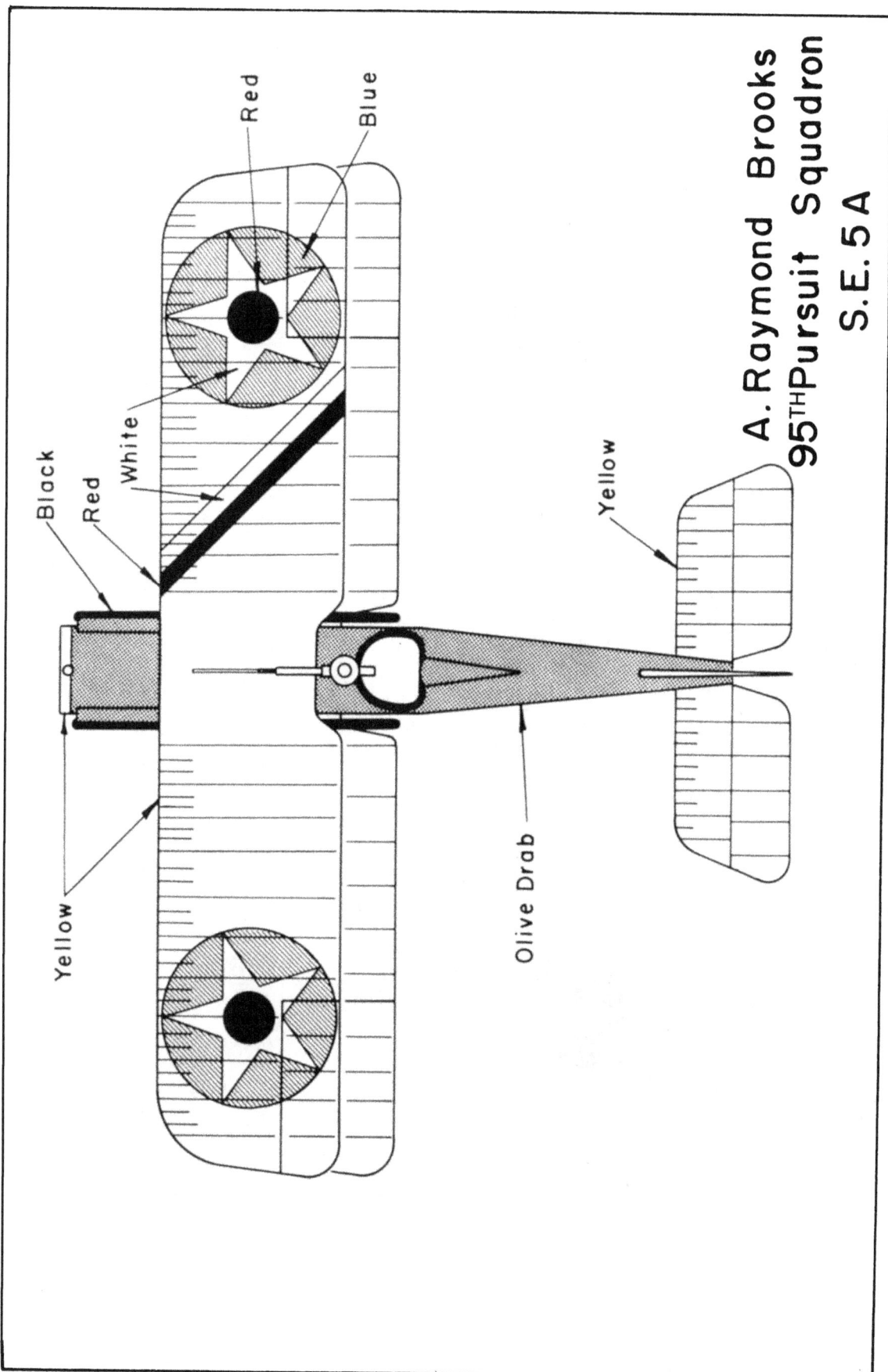

Red

Blue

Red

White

Black

Yellow

Yellow

Olive Drab

A. Raymond Brooks
95TH Pursuit Squadron
S.E.5A

71

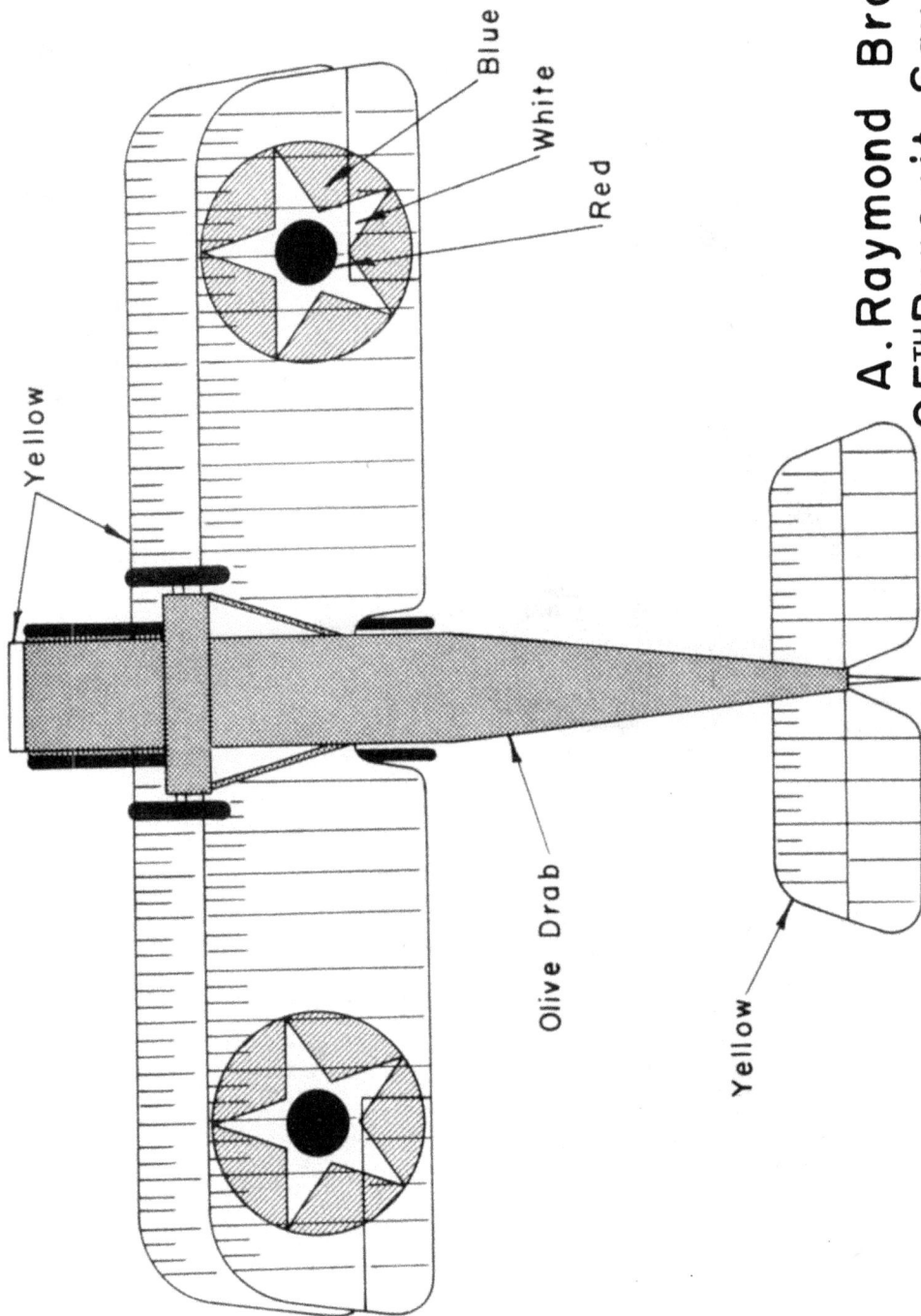

Blue
White
Red

Yellow

Olive Drab

Yellow

A. Raymond Brooks
95TH Pursuit Squadron
S.E.5A

www.ingramcontent.com/pod-product-compliance
Lightning Source LLC
Chambersburg PA
CBHW081300040426
42452CB00014B/2578

9 781479 427925